The first bicy⟨...⟩
ning of the nir⟨...⟩
until the 1890s that the craz⟨...⟩
This brought with it the fears, scaremonger-
ing, worries and uncertainties that inevitably
accompany any new fashion. Women (often
unchaperoned and oddly dressed) taking to
"velocipedes"; over-exertion; the possibility of heart disease—these are just some of
the fears that haunted the establishment in
the late nineteenth century... But with it,
of course, came the joy and wonder of "the
easy and agreeable motion" of this thoroughly
modern means of locomotion.

The books in "Found on the Shelves" have been chosen to give a fascinating insight into the treasures that can be found while browsing in The London Library. Now celebrating its 175th anniversary, with over seventeen miles of shelving and more than a million books, The London Library has become an unrivalled archive of the modes, manners and thoughts of each generation which has helped to form it.

From essays on dieting in the 1860s to instructions for gentlewomen on trout-fishing, from advice on the ill health caused by the "modern" craze of bicycling to travelogues from Norway, they are as readable and relevant today as they were more than a century ago— even if the cardiovascular dangers of cycling have now been disproved!

CYCLING

The Craze of the Hour

The London Library

Pushkin Press

Pushkin Press
71–75 Shelton Street
London WC2H 9JQ

Extract from Charles Spencer, *The Modern Bicycle: containing
Instructions for Beginners; Choice of a Machine; Hints on Training;
Road Book for England and Wales*. London: F. Warne, 1877

Introduction from George Herschell, *Cycling as a Cause of Heart
Disease*. London: Baillière, Tindall and Cox, 1896

Barry Pain, "His Last Pupil" from *Humours of Cycling*. London: Chatto
& Windus, 1905

Jerome K. Jerome, "Women and Wheels" from *Humours of Cycling*.
London: Chatto & Windus, 1905

"A Warning to Enthusiasts" by Edward Tennyson Reed (1860–1933),
published in *Punch; or, The London Charivari*, July 6, 1889

First published by Pushkin Press in 2016

9 8 7 6 5 4 3 2

ISBN 978 1 782272 46 5

Set in Goudy Modern by Tetragon, London

Printed by CPI Group (UK) Ltd, Croydon, CR0 4YY

www.pushkinpress.com

THE MODERN BICYCLE

CONTAINING:

Instructions for Beginners;
Choice of a Machine;
Hints on Training

With Practical Illustrations

BY CHARLES SPENCER, 1877

CHARLES SPENCER owned a shop on Old Street selling equipment for the building of gymnasia. He devoted most of his writing to the subject of cycling, and was heavily involved in the Middlesex Bicycle Club. On 17th February 1869 he rode his bicycle from Trafalgar Square in London to Brighton in just fifteen hours.

Preface

The wonderful transformation undergone by the Bicycle since its introduction, a few years ago, having rendered any previous work upon it quite out of date, I have attempted, in the present, to give a few instructions suited to the new style of machine, and hope they may be useful to our constantly increasing friends, and receive as favourable acceptance as my former little volumes.

2 Old Street, E.C.,
July, 1876.

Introduction

"What makes him go sideways?" was the question addressed by Mr. Snodgrass to Mr. Winkle on his tall bony steed, in the memorable journey of the immortal quartette to Dingley Dell, described in the "Pickwick Papers"; and as any one crossing a bicycle for the first time would feel something of Mr. W.'s awkwardness, and from exactly the same cause—want of skill in riding—I am about to give a few simple instructions for learners, with the view of enabling them to get some command of their iron (or *steel*) steed at an earlier period than they would be able to do by themselves, as I well remember my own early experiences, and can heartily sympathize with their difficulties.

And as I had the principal share in the first introduction of the bicycle a few years ago, and have kept pace with its various stages of improvement up to the present time, it is easy for me to explain and illustrate the enormous difference between riding the early machines and those of the present day; and the contrast between them is really so marked that it is visible to the most ordinary observer. It is difficult to realize the fact that the low clumsy affairs first introduced have developed into the light and graceful machines of the present day. But the simple fact is, that if the present style of bicycle had been brought forward in the first instance, its form would actually have *hindered* and stood in the way of its own success, as it would have been impossible for any one to have *learned* upon it, and in consequence it is probable not one in a hundred of our present numerous riders would have been able to master it.

And although I must certainly plead guilty to being agreeably surprised at the wonderful improvement in the bicycle itself, I must claim to have always recognized its *capability*, and to have had a firm belief in the steady increase in the number of riders. And as it has now gone successfully through the various stages of being laughed at as a *toy*, and tolerated as an amusement, so I am firmly of the opinion that it will eventually become generally useful as a means of *locomotion*.

And as we have various kinds of riding-horses for different purposes, from the roadster to the race-horse, so we have naturally machines of different construction, adapted to the use they are intended for. And here let me make a remark about bicycle *racing*. It is sometimes asked, what is the good of riding at full speed round and round a smooth and level cinder path, when the true use is to travel along turnpike and other roads—good, bad, and indifferent? But, as the race-horse is the highest development of that noble animal, so the racing bicycle is the best form of machine for *speed* which is the primary object in each case; and, of course, it is highly interesting to know the greatest distance that can be run in a given time. And we should no more think of habitually careering along a heavy turnpike road on a racing machine than on a veritable race-horse.

There is no necessity for me to go into a detailed account of the various stages of improvement which the bicycle has gone through, or to give an elaborate description of the first "hobby-horses," "tricycles," &c., &c., or a long and tedious narrative telling who enlarged the fore wheel and diminished the hind one, or to whom we are indebted for steel spider-wheels and india-rubber tyres. This has been done at length by some writers, and any one who wishes can find out these particulars for himself. We have to do with the machine as it is now; and my object is to produce a small handy volume, which may be easily carried in the pocket, containing a few plain instructions for learners and as to the choice of a bicycle, a few hints on training—not special, but suitable for general adaptation—and a comprehensive road book, as the true use of the machine is for travelling far and wide through the country.

And here I may remark that, whereas it was formerly looked upon as a great achievement to run to Brighton in a day, it is now thought nothing very extraordinary to go there and back in the same time.

Lessons in Bicycle-Riding

In the little work I brought out some six or seven years ago (which contained the first instructions for learners ever published), I pointed out the necessity of getting one of the old construction to begin upon; these may be got at a reasonable price, as many have been discarded for the modern ones. They are called "practises," or, more familiarly, "bone-shakers." In learning to ride, it is advisable to have a competent teacher, who can not only show what is wanted, but can also put the beginner in the way of doing it himself; but as many may be unable, from distance or other causes, to avail themselves of this kind of assistance, the following instructions are intended for those who are thus thrown upon their own resources. Of course it is necessary to have recourse to a friendly arm, and there may be many cases in which *two* friends are desirous to learn the bicycle, and can give mutual help.

In the early illustrations, it will be seen that the bicycle is of this construction, that is, of moderate height and the most solid build, and altogether very different from its latest development, as shown in the later sketches, with its enormous driving-wheel and general lightness of make. These machines, with comparatively little difference in the height of the wheel, are best for beginners, as, being *low*, the getting on and off is easier and safer, and they are in every way adapted for the purpose; and it is only when tolerable command of this kind is acquired, that the modern large-wheeled bicycle may be adventured with fair prospect of success.

But even with these some discrimination is necessary. In choosing a machine on which to begin practising, I strongly advise the learner to select one of the size suitable to his height, as, if it is too small, his knees will knock against the handles, and if too large, his legs will not be long enough fairly to reach the throw of the crank. I know it is not uncommon to begin with a boy's machine, and on an inclined plane; but the benefit of these is very doubtful, unless you are totally without help, and have no one to lend you a helping hand.

The best guide in measuring oneself for a bicycle to learn on is, I consider, to stand by its side and see that the saddle is in a line with the hips. The point of the saddle should be about six inches from the upright which supports the handles; for if the saddle is placed too far back, you decrease your power over the driving-wheel, especially in ascending a hill.

When you have secured a good velocipede, well suited to your size, you will find it useful to practise wheeling it slowly along while holding the handles. While thus leading it about, of course you will soon perceive the fact that the first desideratum is to keep the machine perfectly upright, which is done by turning the handles to the right or left when there is any inclination to deviate from the perpendicular. If inclining to the right, turn the wheel *in the same direction*, and *vice versâ*, as it is only the rapidly advancing motion that keeps it upright, on the principle of the boy's hoop (so often quoted), which, the faster it rolls, the better it keeps its perpendicular, and which, when losing its momentum, begins to oscillate, and finally must fall on one side or the other.

Now for the—

First Lesson

Having become accustomed to the motion of the machine, and well studied its mode of travelling, the next thing is to get the assistant to hold it steady while you get astride, and then let him slowly wheel it along.

Fig. 1: How to commence practice

Do not attempt at first to put your feet on the treadles, but let them hang down, and simply sit quiet on the saddle, and take hold of the handles, while the assistant moves you slowly along, with one hand on your arm and the other on the end of the spring, as in Fig. I.

It is hardly necessary to say that the best place to learn is a large room or gallery, with smooth boarded floor or flagstone pavement.

Now, directly you are in motion you will feel quite helpless, and experience a sensation of being run away with, and it will seem as if the machine were trying to throw you off; but all you have to do is to keep the front wheel straight with the back wheel by means of the handles, and the assistant will keep you up and wheel you about for a quarter of an hour or so, taking rest at intervals. When you want to turn, move the handle so as to turn the front wheel in the direction required, but avoid turning too quickly, or you will fall off the reverse way.

Observe that, in keeping your balance, all is done by the hands guiding the front wheel. Do not attempt to sway your body, and so preserve your balance, but sit upright, and if you feel yourself falling to the left, turn the wheel to the *left*; that is to say, guide the machine in the direction in which you are falling, and it will bring you up again; but this must be done the *same moment* you feel any inclination from the perpendicular. Do not be violent and turn the wheel too much, or you will overdo it, and cause it to fall the other way.

Practise guiding the machine in this way until you feel yourself able to be left to yourself for a short distance, and then let the assistant give you a push, and leaving his hold, let you run by yourself for a few yards before you incline to fall. Should you feel that you are losing your balance, stretch out the foot on the side on which you incline, so that you may pitch upon it, and thus arrest your fall.

Second Lesson

Having pretty well mastered the balancing and keeping the machine straight, you may now take a further step, and venture to place your feet on the treadles (as in Fig. 2), and you will now find the novel movement of the legs up and down liable to distract your attention from the steering or balancing; but after a few turns you will get familiarized with the motion, and find this difficulty disappear; and it will seem within the bounds of possibility that you may some time or other begin to travel without assistance.

Fig. 2: Lacing your feet on the treadles

Of course in this and in the former lesson some will take to it more quickly than others, and the duration of the lessons must depend on the learner himself, and the amount of mechanical aptitude which he may be gifted with. Some I have known to take six times as much teaching as others; and I have had the honour of teaching many, and among them some who bear eminent names, M.P.s, bankers, literary men, &c., &c.

Third Lesson

Now, having in the first lesson ridden with
the feet hanging down, and in the second with
them on the treadles, in the third lesson you
should be able to go along for a short distance,
working the treadles in the usual way.

Of course when I speak of the *first* and
second lessons, I do not mean that after practising each of them *once* you will be able, of
necessity, to ride at the *third* attempt, although
I have taught some who seemed to take to it
all at once; but that these are the progressive
steps in learning to ride, and you must practise
each of them until tolerably proficient.

When you are sufficiently familiar with
the working of the treadles while held by the
assistant, it depends entirely on yourself, and
the amount of confidence you may possess, to
determine the time at which he may let go his
hold of you, and you may begin to go alone; but
of course for some time it will be advisable for
him to walk by your side, to catch you in case
of falling. When you have arrived at this stage,

you only require practice to make a good rider, and the amount of practice taken is generally a guide to the amount of skill gained.

To Get On and Off

Having now learnt to ride the velocipede without assistance, we will now proceed to getting on and off in a respectable manner, in case you have not a step, which all modern machines are now provided with. The proper way is to vault on and off, which is the easiest way of all, *when you can do it*, but it certainly requires a little courage and skill.

At first, it may be from want of confidence in yourself, you will jump *at* the machine and knock it over, both you and it coming down. But what is required to be done is, to stand on the *left*-hand side of the bicycle, and throw your *right* leg over the saddle. Stand close to the machine, holding the handles firmly; then run a few steps with it to get a sufficient momentum, and then, leaning your body well over the handles, and throwing as much of your weight as you can upon them, with a slight jump throw your right leg over the saddle.

This may sound formidable, but it is in reality no more than most equestrians do every time they mount, as the height of the bicycle to be cleared is little more than that of the horse's back when the foot is in the stirrup, only the horse is supposed to stand quiet, and therefore you can jump with a kind of swing.

You must be very careful that while running by the side you keep the machine perfectly upright, particularly at the moment of jumping. Perhaps at first you will vault on, forgetting to keep the machine quite perpendicular, and as an inevitable consequence you will come to the ground again, either on your own side, or, what is worse, you may go right over it, and fall with it on the top of you on the *other* side.

Of course it is much better to have an assistant with you at your first attempts at vaulting, and it is good practice to let him hold the machine steady while you vault on and off as many times as you can manage. You must not forget to put all the weight you can on the handles, and although at first this seems difficult, it is comparatively easy when the knack is acquired.

You will not attempt any vaulting until you can manage the machine pretty well when you are on, up to which time the assistant should help you on and set you straight.

To get on with the help of the *treadle* is a very neat and useful method, but requires considerably more practice than vaulting.

Fig. 3: How to get on by the treadle

Stand, as in Fig. 3, with the left foot on the treadle, and taking a slight spring or "beat" from the ground with the right foot, give the machine a good send forward, of course following it yourself, and with a rise bring the right foot over to the saddle. The secret of this movement is that you put as little weight as you can on the treadle, merely following the movement, which has a tendency to lift you, and keep the greater part of your weight on the *handles*.

You may mount the bicycle in another way, and that is by running by its side, and watching the time when one of the treadles is at its lowest (as in Fig. 3); then place your foot upon it, and as it comes up, the momentum thus gained will be sufficient to lift you quite over on to the saddle. In this movement also, as in most others, it is much better to have assistance at first.

To vault off, you have merely to reverse all the movements just described.

Another capital way of alighting from the machine while in motion (Fig. 4) is to throw the right leg over the handles. You hold the left handle firmly, and raise your right leg over and into the centre of the handles, previously raising your right hand to allow the leg to pass under. Then lifting your *left* hand (as in Fig. 4) for the same purpose, you will be able to bring your leg over into a side-sitting posture, and drop on to the ground with the same movement.

Fig. 4: How to alight

But at this time pay strict attention to the *steering*, and take care never to let go one hand until you have a firm hold with the other, or you and the whole affair may come to extreme grief.

This I consider one of the easiest methods of getting off, although it looks so difficult.

To Ride Side-Saddle

Riding in a side-sitting position is very simple, but you must first learn the foregoing exercises.

Fig. 5: To ride side-saddle

First vault on in the usual way, and work up to a moderate speed, then throw the right leg over the handles as in the act of getting off, but still retain your seat, and continue working with the left leg only. Now from this position (Fig. 5) you may practise passing the right leg back again into its original position when sitting across the saddle in the usual way.

To Rest the Legs

Fig. 6 shows a very useful position when taking long journeys, as it rests the legs, and also, as sometimes you do not require to work the treadle descending an incline, the weight of the machine and yourself being sufficient to continue the desired momentum.

Fig. 6: To rest the legs

In this position the *break* is generally used; but when putting it on mind you do not turn the handles with *both* hands at once, but turn with one first and then with the other; as, if the spring should be strong, and you attempt to use both hands in turning it, as a matter of course when you let go to take fresh hold the handles will fly *back*, to your great annoyance.

To Ride Without Using the Hands

This is a very pretty and effective performance, but of course it is rather difficult, and requires much practice before attempting it, as the *steering* must be done with the feet alone, the arms being generally folded as in Fig. 7.

Fig. 7: Riding without using hands

To accomplish this feat, you must keep your feet firmly *on* the treadles in the upward as well as the downward movement, taking care not to take them off at all, as you will thereby keep entire command of them, which is absolutely necessary, as in fact they are doing *double* work, both propelling and also steering the machine. You will, as you become expert in this feat, acquire a kind of *clinging* hold of the treadles, which you will find very useful indeed in ascending a hill when you take to outdoor travelling. Fancy riding of this kind must only be attempted on good surfaces.

Description will not assist you much here, but when you attempt it you will soon find out that when riding without using the hands every stroke of the foot, either right or left, must be of the same force, as, if you press heavier on one treadle than on the other, the machine will have a tendency to go in that direction; and thus you must be on the watch to counteract it by a little extra pressure on the other treadle, without giving enough to turn the machine in the reverse direction.

This is all a matter of nice judgment, but when you can do it a very good effect is produced, giving spectators the idea of your complete mastery of the bicycle.

But remember that you must be always ready to seize the handles and resume command if any interruption to your progress presents itself.

To Ride Without Using Legs or Hands

As you can now ride without using the hands, let us now proceed to try a performance which, at first sight, will perhaps seem almost impossible, but which is really not much more difficult than going without hands. This is to get the velocipede up to *full* speed, and then lift your feet off the treadles and place them on each side of the rest (Fig. 8), and when your legs are up in this way, you will find that you can let go the handles and fold your arms, and thus actually ride without using either *legs* or *hands*.

Fig. 8: Riding without using legs or hands

In progressing thus, the simple fact is that you overcome gravity by motion, and the machine cannot fall until the momentum is lost (*vide* boy's hoop as before).

This should only be attempted by an expert rider, who can get up a speed of twelve to fourteen miles per hour, and on a very good surface and with a good run; and, in fact, from this position you may lean back, and lay flat down, your body resting on and along the spring. I know several gentlemen who could run the length of the Agricultural Hall in this way, when that spacious building was used for velocipede-riding.

At Rest

We are now come to the last and best, or, I may say, the most useful feat of all, and this is to stop the bicycle and sit quite still upon it.

The best way to commence practising this is to run into a position where you can hold by a railing or a wall, or perhaps the assistant will stand with his shoulder ready for you to take hold of.

Now gradually slacken speed, and when coming nearly to a standstill, turn the front wheel until it makes an angle of 45 deg. with the back wheel, and try all you know to sit perfectly still and upright, as in Fig. 9.

Fig. 9: At rest

Of course this is a question of balancing, and you will soon find the knack of it. When the machine inclines to the left, slightly press the left treadle, and if it evinces a tendency to lean to the right, press the right treadle; and so on, until, sooner or later, you achieve a correct equilibrium, when you may take out your pocket-book and read or even write letters, &c., without difficulty.

Now, I do not think that there is anything further to be said as to learning to ride the bicycle, and I can only express a hope that if you follow the advice and instruction I have been able to give, you will become an expert rider and be able to begin practising on the "Modern Bicycle."

The Duplex Bicycle

I believe the idea of two men riding on one machine is not novel, but in the drawing before the reader the novelty that is claimed lies in the connecting-iron, by means of which the two front wheels of two ordinary bicycles of the same make may be coupled together, and so formed into the duplex. Thus the expense attending the manufacture of an entirely new machine is avoided, and the purchase of the duplex connecting-iron complete, and one spring alone, is necessary to complete the machine.

Fig. 10

The Duplex is fitted with two brakes, both acting on the rear wheel, and one worked by each handle; two steps, and a leather splasher over the rear wheel to prevent splashing the man riding in front.

Choice of a Machine

And first, as to the choice of a machine. In this case it is imperative to have the very best you can get, as it is utter folly to risk life and limb by using one of inferior make. As I have myself been in the constant habit of riding from its first introduction, and have travelled many thousand miles on machines of all the principal makers, I can speak from my own knowledge when I say that the Coventry Machinists' Company produce the very best machines, both for general riding and racing. From their system of making all the parts of their machines to a gauge (like watches, sewing machines, &c.), it is easy to replace anything that may be damaged or worn out; so that if any part of your machine wants renewing, you can write or telegraph for it from wherever you may happen to be. I fancy that if makers generally adopted this plan, it would be of very great convenience. To any one happening to be in or near Coventry, a visit to their immense works is an interesting and instructive sight; and I am sure that the manager is pleased to show any one interested in bicycling over them. Fig. 11 and 12 represent two of their bicycles—a roadster and a racer.

The world-renowned John Keen, the champion, of Clapham Junction, also turns out first-class racing machines, upon which he has won many important races, and the greatest credit

Fig. 11   *Fig. 12*

is due to him for his continued efforts both as a maker and a rider.

In choosing a bicycle, of course the first thing to be considered is the height of wheel, which greatly depends on the length of limb of the rider; as, of course, although two men may be of equal height, one may have a longer leg than the other. A good guide is to sit on the machine and let the toe touch the lower treadle without quite straightening the leg, as of course command must never be lost. For a rider of average height, say 5 feet 8 inches, a machine of 52 to 54 inches I should consider suitable. But of course any well-known and reliable maker will furnish you with a machine to suit you.

Having selected your "Modern Bicycle," the first thing you want to accomplish is to be able to mount and dismount. Of course, the saddle being nearly as high as your shoulder, it is impossible to vault on, as with the old "practiser." It is therefore necessary to provide a "step," which, in all the modern machines, is fitted on the backbone, or connecting-iron, just above the hinder fork on the left side, at a convenient height. It consists of a small round plate, jagged, to afford a firm grip for the toe when placed upon it.

Fig. 13

There are two ways of mounting. One is to start the machine and to run by the left side, and put the left toe upon the step while in motion, throwing the right leg over on to the seat; the other is to stand at the back of the machine, standing on the right leg, with the left toe on the step (as in Fig. 13), and, gently starting, hop with the right leg until you have gained a sufficient impetus to raise yourself on the step, and throw your right leg across the seat.

Fig. 14

The first is the best plan, as you can run with greater speed, and mount; in fact, the quicker you go, the easier to get on. In many cases it is the only practicable plan, as, for instance, on remounting on a slight ascent, where it would be most difficult to get up sufficient speed by the hopping plan, which, moreover, does not present a very graceful appearance.

Now, in the second way of getting on by the step, as in Fig. 14, you hold the handle with the left hand to guide the machine, placing the other on the seat. You can now run it along easily. Your object in having one hand on the seat is, that if both hands are on the handles, you are over-reached, and it is difficult to keep your balance. Now take a few running steps, and when the right foot is on the ground give a hop with *that* foot, and at the same time place the left foot on the step, throwing your right leg over on to the seat. Now, the *hop* is the principal thing to be done, as if, when running beside the bicycle at a good speed, you were merely to place the left foot on the step without giving a good hop with the other, the right leg would be left behind, and you would be merely what is called "doing the splits."

You will see at once that as the machine is travelling at good speed, you have no *time* to raise one foot after the other (as in walking upstairs), as when you lift up your foot, you are, as it were, "in the air," and nothing but a good long running hop will give time to adjust your toe on the step as it is moving. This is, of course, difficult to describe, and, I need not say, requires a certain amount of strength and agility, without which no one can expect to become an expert rider.

But, in the high racing machines, no one would think of trying to mount without the assistance of a friendly arm, and a stand or stool of suitable height.

Fig. 15

Having now mounted the high machine (Fig. 15), you will find that the reach of the leg, and the position altogether, is very different from the seat on the "bone-shaker"; but when you get some command, you will find the easy gliding motion much pleasanter, as well as faster. You are now seated much higher, in fact, almost on the top of the wheel; and, instead of using the ball of the foot, you must use your toe; and when the treadle is at the bottom of the throw of the crank, your leg will be almost at its fullest extent and nearly straight.

Now you must pay a little attention to the process of alighting.

In getting off by the step all you have to do is to reach back your left foot until you feel the step, and, resting upon the handles, raise yourself up, and throw the right leg over the seat on to the ground.

But I consider getting off by the treadle much the preferable way when you can manage it; but you must be very careful when first trying not to attempt it until the machine is perfectly at rest. Get some one to hold you up, the bicycle being stationary, and practise getting off in the following manner: First, see that the left hand crank is at the bottom, and with your left foot on that treadle practise swinging your right leg backwards and forwards, in order to get used to the movement. Now while in position, as in Fig. 16, throw your right leg with a swing backwards, resting as much as you can of your weight upon the handles, and raise yourself with your right foot into position as in Fig. 17, continuing your swinging movement until you are off the seat and on the ground.

Fig. 16   *Fig. 17*

When you are well able to get off in this way, with the bicycle at rest, you may attempt it when slackening speed to stop. As it is, of course, easier to get off the slower you are going, you must come almost to a standstill, just keeping way enough to prevent the machine falling over, as if you attempt it when going at all quickly, you will have to run by its side after you are off, which is a difficult feat for any but a skilful rider.

The great advantage of getting off in this way is that, with practice, you can choose your own time, which is very useful when an obstacle suddenly presents itself, as in turning a corner; and in getting off the other way you are liable to lose time in feeling for the step.

There are different styles of riding, and of course at first you are glad to be able to get along in any way you can; but when you come to have any command over your machine, and have time to think about *style*, you cannot do better than take for your model John Keen, the champion, whose upright and graceful seat gives such an impression of quiet power. Very different is the appearance presented by some well-known riders, who, although going at really good speed, present a painful appearance, hanging forwards over the handles as if about to topple over, and favouring the beholders with such a variety of facial contortions.

Hints on Training

It is very difficult to give any rules that will apply to all, as constitutions differ so widely; but the simple rules of regular diet, rest, and exercise will apply to every one, whether they are going, as the saying is, "to race for a man's life," or merely trying to get themselves into the best frame of body to endure moderate exertion. The daily use of the cold bath, or tepid if necessary, cannot be too strongly insisted upon; and also early rising and going to rest; and the avoidance of all rich viands, such as pork, veal, duck, salmon, pastry, &c., &c. Beef, mutton, fowls, soles, and fish of a similar kind, should form the principal diet. The severity of the rules of professional training has been much relaxed of late years, and many things, such as vege-tables, stimulants in great moderation, &c.,

are now allowed, which before were rigidly excluded.

In training for any special effort, of course it is necessary to have professional assistance; but with moderate attention to diet and regimen, any one may soon get himself into good condition, and particularly if he becomes an habitual bicycle-rider.

As there may be some of our readers who are inclined to obesity, which will materially interfere with their success in learning to ride, I give an extract from Banting's little work, attention to which will be found of great benefit in reducing fat; bearing in mind that they must be followed intelligently, and only as far as the strength will safely allow.

"The items from which I was advised to abstain as much as possible were:——Bread, butter, milk, sugar, beer, and potatoes, which had been the main (and, I thought, innocent) elements of my subsistence, or at all events they had for many years been adopted freely.

"These, said my excellent adviser, contain starch and saccharine matter, tending to create fat, and should be avoided altogether. At the first blush it seemed to me that I had little left to live upon, but my kind friend soon showed me there was ample. I was only too happy to give the plan a fair trial, and, within a very few days found immense benefit from it. It may better elucidate the dietary plan if I describe generally what I have sanction to take, and that man must be an extraordinary person who would desire a better table:—

"For breakfast, at 9 a.m., I take five to six ounces, of either beef, mutton, kidneys, broiled fish, bacon, or cold meat of any kind except pork or veal; a large cup of tea or coffee (without milk or sugar), a little biscuit, or one ounce of dry toast; making together six ounces solid, nine liquid.

"For dinner, at 2 p.m., five or six ounces of any fish except salmon, herrings, or eels, any meat except pork or veal, any vegetable except potato, parsnip, beetroot, turnip, or carrot, one ounce of dry toast, fruit out of a pudding not sweetened, any kind of poultry or game, and two or three glasses of good claret, sherry, or Madeira: Champagne, port, and beer forbidden; making together ten to twelve ounces solid, and ten liquid.

"For tea, at 6 p.m., two or three ounces of cooked fruit, a rusk or two, and a cup of tea without milk or sugar; making two to four ounces solid, nine liquid.

"For supper, at 9 p.m., three or four ounces of meat or fish, similar to dinner, with a glass or two of claret or sherry and water; making four ounces solid and seven liquid.

"For nightcap, if required, a tumbler of grog—(gin, whisky, or brandy without sugar)—or a glass or two of claret or sherry.

"This plan leads to an excellent night's rest, with from six to eight hours' sound sleep.

"With the dry toast or rusk at breakfast and tea, I generally take a table-spoonful of spirit to soften it, which may prove acceptable to others. Perhaps I do not wholly escape starchy or saccharine matter, but scrupulously avoid milk, sugar, beer, butter, &c., which are known to contain them."

CYCLING AS A CAUSE OF HEART DISEASE

BY GEORGE HERSCHELL, M.D., 1896

Senior Physician to the National Hospital for Diseases of the Heart, etc., Soho Square; Late Physician to the West End Hospital for Diseases of the Nervous System

GEORGE HERSCHELL was a specialist in diseases of the digestive organs, and led a successful life both as a practising doctor and as the writer of medical papers. In his spare time he enjoyed golf and photography. He died in 1914.

RESTORATION OF BRITISH CYCLIST.
20TH CENTURY.   BRITISH MUSEUM.

A WARNING TO ENTHUSIASTS.

Preface

The origin of this short essay was a paper enti-
tled "Cycling as a Cause of Heart Disease"
which was communicated to the Eighth
International Congress of Hygiene and
Demography, held at Budapest in 1894, and
an abstract of which, by the courtesy of the
editors of the *Lancet*, I was enabled to lay
before the medical profession in the issue of
March 2, 1895. Since that time I have been
so frequently asked for further information
on the subject that I have been encouraged to
amplify and rearrange my original paper and
publish it in its present form.

GEORGE HERSCHELL.
27, QUEEN ANNE STREET,
CAVENDISH SQUARE.
NOVEMBER, 1896.

Introduction

It is conceived that hardly any apology is necessary for the appearance of a small work drawing the attention of medical men to one class of affections likely to arise from the immoderate use of cycling, viz., disease of the heart and arteries.

At a moment when old and young and middle-aged are alike resorting to this form of exercise, recreation and locomotion,* a word of warning may not be out of place. Without it, there is some fear that in many cases the craze of the hour may develop into the injury of a lifetime; and those who at the beginning of their cycling career deem they have lighted upon a blessing may live to discover that in their favourite exercise the reverse has been their fate. It has been said before that it is not difficult to find some specious apothegm or aphorism in support of almost any

---

* The total number of cyclists in the United Kingdom has recently been estimated at one and a half million, on the basis that only two and a half per cent. join the G.T.C.

proposition, and if reliance were alone placed on the old German adage of *Zu viel ist unge-sund*, the case against immoderation in cycling would be proved even before it was opened. Unfortunately, or perhaps fortunately, the medical man is not permitted to content him-self with proverbial generalities, and when once he is honestly convinced by study and examination that a real danger looms in view, it is undoubtedly his duty to his fellow practi-tioners to place in detail before them the facts and arguments in support of his belief and the position which they have forced him to take up.

In Nature there seems to be a law of com-pensation. To the artificial life that we lead in our big cities, to the sedentary occupations to which so many of us are forced, we can trace the beginnings and developments of many affections. Insufficient exercise apparently being in most cases the principal factor, we rush to the cycle as an easy, agreeable, and convenient method of undoing or preventing such mischief. What is the consequence? We fall in love with the machine, with its easy and agreeable motion: we give as much of our time to it as we can afford: we get rid of our dyspepsia, and in its place produce chronic degenerative changes in our heart and in our arteries. Indigestion, gout and neurasthenia diminish, only to be replaced by more serious ills; and the physician of a few years hence will have to treat many more cases of chronic disease of the heart and arteries than he does at the present time, simply on account of the immoderate use, or rather abuse, of the cycle by individuals whose tissues are unfit to undergo the strain which this exercise is bound to put upon them.

The answer to this would seem to be that all we have to do is to cycle in moderation, and no doubt it is theoretically, and in some cases practically, possible to cycle in moderation and derive nothing but benefit from so doing. In most instances, however, the contrary is the case. Our first aim in cycling is to pass the novice-state when we feel we overdo it and get knocked up, and to substitute for such distress and exhaustion the sense of physical *bien-aise* of a well-trained man engaged in active work. But if we succeed in attaining this condition we have not really improved our chance of escaping possible heart affection produced by cycling. We have merely altered the kind of affection which we shall produce. And, strange to say, the advantage is apparently not upon the side of the trained man. For whilst the novice by sheer carelessness may strain his heart—but if under middle age can escape if he will only take the most ordinary precautions—the skilled and trained professional cyclist, on the contrary, who can travel for hours without turning a hair, is almost certain to produce degenerative changes in his heart and arteries. Nothing he can do will prevent this happening. For, as he cannot control the amount of blood pressure in his arteries, he is absolutely at the mercy of his own tissues. If these are inherently weak nothing can save him. And if such is the case with a young man who starts his cycling career with a sound heart and healthy arteries, what can we expect of a man who commences to ride at an age when from the ordinary nature of things his tissues must have already undergone a certain amount of deterioration? He is heavily handicapped from the start. It is logically certain that a certain proportion of the men and women over middle age who are now taking up cycling must have degenerating and weak hearts, although they are unaware of the fact. It is simply a question of mathematics. Of a thousand people over middle age, we may expect to find a hundred whose circulatory apparatus is beginning to show signs of wear. If only fifty out of this thousand take up cycling—and as things go I am sure this is below the average—out of this fifty, five will certainly have affected hearts. And there is no getting away from this fact. It therefore follows that at least five out of every fifty persons over middle age who take up cycling will be almost certain to do themselves grave injury unless they exercise the greatest prudence. Again, in addition to those who take to cycling because it is fashionable, many do so in the hope of curing indigestion, gout, and other ills. We must bear in mind that those very symptoms which the patient imagines are due to dyspepsia may really be the first insidious symptoms of heart disease. Dyspepsia is not a disease; it is a collection of symptoms pointing to disease somewhere, and one cause not uncommon and frequently overlooked is weakness of the heart. The middle-aged man suffers from symptoms of an indefinite nature. He is troubled with flatulence both before and after meals. He is short of breath on slight exertion and has palpitation of the heart. His sleep is broken and disturbed, and he probably dreams. He may occasionally feel a little faint or have attacks of pain in the chest. When he consults a capable medical man he learns to his surprise that his heart is unsound. We can easily imagine what will be the result if he takes to vigorous cycling under the impression that he is merely suffering from indigestion, and that active exercise will prove a sovereign cure. As regards gout, since this complaint is so frequently associated with atheroma of the arteries, it necessarily follows that a certain number of those who take to cycling to cure their gout will have this arterial condition. To these the increased blood-pressure which of necessity accompanies a long ride on the cycle at any except a very moderate pace must be highly dangerous. It can do them nothing but good to potter about the park or a country road, but they ride at the risk of their life unless they do so at a very moderate pace and when using a low gear. For not only are they incurring the risk of fatal syncope, a Nemesis common to all who put an abnormal strain upon a degenerated heart or vessels, but there is always the chance of the giving way of an atheromatous artery in the brain, or even of rupture of the heart itself.

The cyclists who habitually ride long distances must now be considerable. The number of individuals who make a profession of cycling is rapidly increasing, particularly that class who travel over the country attending meetings. These will average two or three races a week for six months in the year; and as they are handicapped according to their form and previous performances, such races are usually hotly contested. Among amateurs, every large club has its record for long distances against time. We have what is known as the "maker's amateur" always with us.

It is an open question whether we should allow little children to cycle. They are all eager to do so as they see their elders crazed upon the subject, and the cycle manufacturers are fostering the idea by placing on the market diminutive wheels. Of course cycling for very short distances with low gear and frequent rests can do a child no manner of harm. But to ensure this, constant supervision is necessary. My experience is that when a boy learns cycling he does *not* confine himself to what would be harmless to him, but is even more inclined to overdo it than grown-up people. When out with a party he will of necessity have to keep up with his elders, and when alone he tries to break records. The average boy has very lofty ideals in the way of athletics. I would say that these statements of mine are not purely theoretical. Among others, I knew a boy of ten who used to ride to Brighton and back, and accompanied his father on all his excursions. I read in the cycling papers quite recently of a little boy who, at the mature age of four, has taken to the path. What effect will the continuous high pressure in the arteries of this infant have upon the development of his circulatory system? Time only will show. We have at present no data upon which to form an opinion, as it is probably the first time in the history of the world that the problem has been presented to us, and that anything like cycling has become a factor in the evolution, development and growth of our children. *When we allow a child to ride long distances upon a cycle we are carrying out a physiological experiment which, although possibly of interest from a scientific standpoint, must be utterly unjustifiable.*

The amount of disease which will be produced by cycling in the near future rests with that large body of family physicians in this country, whom I am addressing in this essay.

They must insist upon making a thorough examination of the heart of every patient over middle age who may be taking up cycling. Not merely a casual auscultation, which too often passes for an examination of the heart, but a careful estimation by inspection, palpation, and percussion, of the position of the apex beat, diffusion, extent, and character of the impulse, and the area of deep cardiac dullness. By auscultation, the character, force, and rhythm of the heart sounds must be carefully studied, the examiner bearing in mind that there may be serious degeneration of the heart-muscle without any murmur. He must also remember that whilst in children and young adults the heart affection is, as a rule, more or less acute and obvious, after middle age the type changes, and we shall then find slow and insidious changes in the substance of which the heart and arteries are composed, and primary degenerations.

The pulse must be also thoroughly studied, with the especial object of determining the condition of the arterial walls and the degree of tension. For this purpose I can strongly recommend the routine use of the sphygmograph.

Having made such an examination the practitioner will be in the position to allow the patient to cycle without restraint, or to put an absolute veto upon this form of exercise, or to lay down rules for its safe indulgence; and to prescribe the daily amount, the pace, and other details which may enable the patient to use the cycle not only with impunity but even with advantage.

On his part every intending cyclist will be well advised if he consult his medical adviser and be thoroughly overhauled before commencing to learn.

HIS LAST PUPIL

BY BARRY PAIN, 1905

BARRY PAIN is best remembered for his "Eliza"
stories; he was known during his lifetime as a
writer of parody and lightly humorous stories. He
was an eccentric man, with such varied interests as
Georgian literature, the occult and precious stones.

"'The best thing you can do,' said my
doctor, 'is to take to bicycling.'"

"**T**he best thing you can do," said my doctor, "is to take to bicycling."

"At present, of course, one bicycles," said the man of the world.

"You're missing the finest possible enjoyment by not bicycling," said my athletic friend.

In fact, wherever I went I was met by bicyclists who longed to make others bicycle. It was not for health, nor for fashion, nor for exercise that I finally took to the machine; it was simply from the pressure of public opinion. When I had finally given in, and made up my mind to spoil my clothes, bruise my body, and ruin my temper by learning to ride, I sought out my athletic friend, and asked him to tell me if there was any instructor whom he could especially recommend.

"Yes," he said, "there is. There is one man, Barkinstone by name, who has quite a small shop in the Enderdown Road. He knows more about the bike than any two other men in England put together. I would not dream of buying a new machine myself without consulting Barkinstone about it, though he would charge me a guinea for his opinion."

I said that that seemed rather a lot of money.

My friend confessed that it was so. "But if you want the very best, you always have to pay for it. Barkinstone's thorough, that's what he is. He never advertises, and never makes any fuss, but on his merits alone he always has more work than he can do. He never employs an assistant—except of course in his workshops. If he consents to teach you, he will charge you £5, no matter how few or how many lessons you may require. It seems a good deal of money, I daresay, but then remember that if you pay for Barkinstone you get Barkinstone. He does not hand you over to some understrapper who knows nothing of the real science of the thing. And he will turn you out perfect. Your style will be absolutely correct; you will ride easily and confidently; you will thoroughly understand the mechanism of your bike, and if any trifling accident occurs, be able to put it right for yourself instead of rushing off to a repairer. Don't do it unless you like, but if you do, I can guarantee that you will get your money's worth."

"Did he teach you?" I asked.

"Well, I'll tell you. I learned to ride all right, as I thought then, from a friend of mine. After I had ridden for about a year, I met one of Barkinstone's pupils, a lady, and when I watched her I felt dissatisfied with myself and uneasy about my riding. I got an introduction from her—he won't take a pupil without an introduction—and went to Barkinstone. 'Look here,' I said, 'I want you to try me and see if I ride properly.' He put me a lot of tests, and I thought I got through most of them fairly well. 'Yes,' said Barkinstone, 'your machine doesn't suit you, and your saddle's not right. You get along, anyhow, and ride like the average man.' 'What do I want?' I asked. 'Two finishing lessons at a guinea each,' he said. I took them, and I never spent money better. Gained

*"He was a tall, thin man, with a loose
lip and an enquiring eye."*

in comfort, gained in speed, and got an understanding of the machine that was alone worth the money."

That decided me. With an introduction from my athletic friend, I sought out Barkinstone in the Enderdown Road. He was a tall, thin man, with a loose lip and an enquiring eye. He heard what I wanted, and then looked up entries in a note-book. "I'm full up for a fortnight," he said. "You can take the course then if you like. I shall require the five pounds paid in advance, and a written promise to keep my system of tuition secret. That is my usual custom." I gave him the money and the promise, and said good morning.

"Wait a minute, sir," said Barkinstone. "I must have a machine exactly right ready for you to learn on. Step this way." He took me into another room, weighed me carefully, measured me frequently and accurately, and told me exactly what clothes I was to get. He had a model suit there, and explained it to me. He had a tame tailor, who was entrusted with the making of these suits; he would not risk his secret by allowing you to employ your own tailor.

At the end of a fortnight I returned to him.

*   *   *

I paid altogether (exclusive of a moderate charge for the clothes) eight pounds three shillings to Barkinstone: five pounds for tuition, one guinea for choosing a machine for me, and two guineas for procuring, altering, and fitting a special saddle. In four days I could ride straight up a stiff hill, without bending my back, and with my hands off. I could take my machine to pieces and put it together again. On the fifth day I rode forty miles without feeling particularly exhausted. Now I am by no means an athlete, and I am particularly slow at learning anything. In short, Barkinstone was expensive, but he was also the most amazingly clever and thorough instructor that the world has yet produced. I sent him four pupils, and the last of them had to wait three months before Barkinstone could take him.

At a rough guess, I should say that Barkinstone was making from fifty to sixty pounds a week clear profit. I heard indirectly that he was investing largely in house property.

* * *

About a year after this, I was in a fishing village on the Yorkshire coast. I was there for a holiday, and (like most writing men) found that I got rather more work done in my holiday than I did any other time. One very hot day I had been sitting out in the garden most of the morning and afternoon, doing bad reviews of worse novels at my leisure. After dinner, I finished the reviews and took them out to the post. I observed that there was a glorious full moon, that the roads were in capital condition; and I remembered that I had taken no exercise all day. I went back to the house, brought out my bicycle, lit a totally unnecessary but strictly legal lamp, and rode off. The first few miles I went slowly with my

"I settled down to some good hard work."

hands in my pockets; then I settled down to some good hard work. I had not taken any particular note of the direction in which I was going, nor how long I had been riding, when I thought I heard a village clock in the distance strike one. Then I glanced at my watch, and found that it was indeed an hour after midnight. I decided to ride on to the village, and then turn back and go home. The road here stretched long and white. On one side was the low stone wall of a park, on the other was a steep downward slope covered with grass and brambles. I noticed in the distance a tiny spark darting hither and thither, occasionally stopping suddenly and then zig-zagging again. As I came nearer, I perceived that this spark was a bicycle lamp, and that the machine was being ridden by someone not expert, someone who occasionally collapsed and desperately remounted. Nearer still I drew; the other cyclist was visible now, his shoulders hunched, his knees turned in, and his insteps well over the pedals. I prepared to dodge, and it was as well I did for just as we met he gave another

"He went bang into the wall."

lurch and came at me. I escaped him, and he went bang into the wall, shoved himself off with one hand, shot across to the other side of the road, and tumbled straight down the embankment. Then from motives of humanity I got off my machine. I called down the embankment, "Are you hurt?"

After a moment a voice came from the middle of a bramble-bush:

"Not much. The bike's—er—rather entangled. But I can manage—don't stop for me."

However, I leant my machine against the wall, took off the lamp, and climbed down the embankment with it in my hand. Against the bramble-bush was the rider, stooping down and rubbing his shins. Beside him was a lump of mixed machinery that had once been a bicycle. He looked up as I approached, and the light of my lamp fell full on his face.

"Barkinstone!" I exclaimed. "Barkinstone of the Enderdown Road, by all that's miraculous!"

"No, no," he said; "my name is— er—Brown."

"Not a bit of it," I replied. "You taught me to ride, and I know you. You're Barkinstone."

"I knew this would happen one of these days," he said to himself mournfully. "Yes, sir, it's no good to say otherwise. I'm Barkinstone."

"And the amazing part of it is, you don't talk in the least as if you were drunk."

"I'm not drunk. I know my business well enough—see—look at this." He took a couple of tools from his pocket. Then he picked up a bundle of spokes, some scraps of tyre, a handle-bar, and what was left of the saddle, and in a very few minutes had made a bicycle out of them. "There, does that look as if I were drunk?"

"No," I said, "it doesn't. And, drunk or sober, nobody but you could have done it. But why did you ride like that?"

"Because I can't ride any better. In fact, that ride to-night was the best I've ever done. I've never been so far before without falling off."

"Still I don't understand. You taught me to ride. You have taught hundreds to ride."

"Yes; but I can't teach myself."

"You have a theory of riding that is absolutely correct. It has been tested."

"Yes, the theory's correct in nine hundred and ninety-nine cases out of a thousand. I'm the thousandth. Was I riding properly when you saw me?"

"You were pedalling very unevenly and badly; you clung hard to the handles; you kept looking at the front wheel; you——"

"Oh, you needn't go on! I was doing everything that I oughtn't to do. I know it. The theory fails with me, because I am the thousandth case. Do you think it takes any courage to learn to ride the bicycle?"

"None whatever—not in the least."

"I'll put it in a different way. Can you conceive of a want of nerve so terrible, a physical cowardice so great, that it might absolutely prevent a man from learning to bike—or at any rate cause him to take years over it, where other men would only take days?"

"No, I can't."

"Very likely not, sir. But I suffer from just that want of nerve, just that physical

"Came down in the road with the machine on top of him."

cowardice. I stand beside the machine, and my nerve's all right, and I know all there is to know about riding. I've only got to put my foot on the step, and my nerve's gone, and in a moment I've forgotten everything; then I flounder about—and come off—and hurt myself—and break things."

He limped up the embankment to the road, carrying his machine and refusing any assistance.

"Going to get on again?" I asked.

"Oh, yes! I've got perseverance and moral courage, if I haven't got physical courage and nerve."

He placed his left foot on the step, propelled the machine in a slow curve with three convulsive kicks with his right foot, rose slowly into the air, then slipped off the step and came down in the road with the machine on top of him. He was apparently quite used to this kind of thing, for he observed in an unmoved voice from under the machine, "There was one thing I forgot to mention, sir."

"Well, what was it?"

"You would do me a great favour," he said, rising slowly, "if you would for the present keep this incident a secret. You know what the public is, sir. If the public knew that I could not ride, it would never believe that I could teach other people to ride. I am about to retire; in another six months I shall be able to give up the business, and live in comfort in a fine house in the country for the rest of my days. After that, it doesn't much matter what you say, for no pupil has ever been dissatisfied with me. But, until then, it might spoil business."

"But why give up your business? You're far too young a man to retire. What interest have you got in the country? What would you do with yourself?"

"Learn the bicycle. I shall be my own pupil. It will take me all my life. Good-night, sir... Well, thanks, if you'd just give me a hand."

He relit his lamp. I held the machine while he mounted, and then shoved him off. He vanished like a diamond-pointed corkscrew, more or less in the direction of the village.

He has retired now. The grounds of his country house are secluded by high walls. I am told that, inside, an asphalt track has been constructed. It hurts to fall on asphalt.

WOMEN AND WHEELS

BY JEROME K. JEROME, 1897

As well as writing this short story, the successful author also wrote *Three Men on the Bummel*, an unsuccessful sequel to *Three Men in a Boat*, in which the same characters, minus the dog, go on a cycling tour through the Black Forest. He died in 1927.

I met Moore on Tuesday in Pall Mall, and asked him how his wife was. He said he did not know, he had not seen her for ten days.

"Dear me," I said, "and you used to be so fond of one another. Can nothing be done?"

"Nothing," he groaned. I walked with him a little way, pondering how to advise him.

"Do you know where she is?" I asked.

"I am not certain," he replied, "but I expect"——he took out his watch and looked at it. It was five minutes past eleven——"I expect she's in Battersea Park."

"It's not very far," I said. "Why don't you go and fetch her out?"

"It would be no good," he argued; "she wouldn't come."

I glanced at him sharply. I began to fear that he was what Arthur Roberts would call "dotty on the bun." His pale, set face belied my suspicions, however, so I spoke kindly to him.

"Why don't you go down," I urged, "and see what can be done? You have only been married eighteen months. She can't have ceased to care for you altogether."

"I have been," he answered. "I followed her for miles. Don't ask me to go again; I can't bear it."

The New Woman is difficult to fathom. You have to be prepared for everything. I could understand her running away from a loving husband after a few months of wedded bliss, but why to Battersea Park! It seemed an inadequate place as a refuge for a disappointed woman. I was curious on the subject.

"What was she doing there?" I asked.

The man's whole frame seemed torn by emotion. "She's there," he replied hoarsely, "with a man named McGunnis. They walk slowly up and down with their arms round each other's waists. In moments of deep feeling she flings her arms round his neck, and cries to him before all the spectators not to desert her. He takes her in his arms and comforts her with tender, reassuring words."

We had reached the Reform Club. Moore leant against the stuccoed balustrade for support.

"And it's not always McGunnis," he continued. "On Mondays and Wednesdays it's a man named Stendall. He's a married man with eight children; anything does for her. This thing is undermining the femininity of the nation."

I began to comprehend the matter; Moore views life from a serious standpoint.

"Oh, come," I said, "you mustn't take on about it; they all do it."

"I know they all do it," he replied fiercely; "does that make it any the better? Aunt Jane does it—you know Aunt Jane?"

I replied that I did. I must confess it surprised me to hear that his Aunt Jane did it. She is a heavily built, elderly lady, of strongly pronounced Evangelical views. She is not the sort of person one would imagine giving way to it.

"She goes out late at night with a fellow named Hockey," said Moore; "she's old enough to be his mother. They pick out all the darkest streets. Of course they have a lamp, but it's only half a candle power, and all the light is in front. It's impossible to see what goes on behind it. I call it disgraceful!"

I took him into the club and gave him a brandy and soda. He confided to me that he had lost four pairs of trousers in the last fortnight.

"They wear them underneath their skirts," he explained; "but that is only for practice. You mark my words, there will come a day when they will wear them openly. I tell you this thing is interfering with religion." He drew his chair closer, and whispered to me,—

"Can you imagine Aunt Jane in rationals?"

"She has hardly the figure for it," I replied.

"Hardly!" he cried. "How much more do you think she wants? She wears them in the house to get used to them, and if Providence in its mercy doesn't interfere and kill her off quietly in a dark street—about which I have hopes—you will see her riding in them in Hyde Park!"

I tried to chaff him into taking a lighter view of the matter, but without success.

Outside the club steps was a lady's bicycle, propped up against a lamp-post. I left him standing before it silently cursing it. His expression was prophetic, and the bicycle—it was a poor specimen—struck me as looking shamed.

The next afternoon I met little Rogers, of *The Standard*, with a black eye. The cricket season not having commenced, I felt justified in asking for an explanation.

"I have been teaching the wife bicycling," he said.

"But why did she hit you in the eye?" I inquired; "you were doing your best, weren't you?"

"She did it with the bicycle," he said.

"Yes, it looks a nasty one," I answered. "Are you going to summons her?"

"Oh, no," he replied meekly; "it was quite an accident. It was really my fault. I fell down, and she rode over me."

"She seems pretty expert," I said.

"Oh, yes," he agreed; "she's getting on nicely. She will be finished soon."

"Well, take care you're not finished first," I advised him; "it seems a dangerous job."

"It is ticklish work," he assented, "but I am getting more careful. The great thing," he explained, "is to be there when you're wanted, and not to be there when you're not wanted, if you understand."

I said I thought I did, and left him.

Every woman in London, apparently, is learning to ride the bicycle. The streets and parks echo to the cries of "I'm going, I'm going, hold me back!"—"You're all right, I've got you."—"Oh, don't leave me, I can't."— "Yes you can, mind the kerb. Don't look at your feet, you can't fall."—"Oh dear, what's happened?"—"It's all right."—"There you are, I knew it!"—"Oh, that's nothing, you'll get used to that. Jump up."

Mingled with the women are many middle-aged and elderly gentlemen, short of wind but earnest of purpose. From inquiries I have made, I gather that, taking the average, a person can learn the bicycle in six months, provided they don't miss a single day. The lessons last about half an hour, and the charge is from half a crown to five shillings. Indeed, I have serious thoughts of abandoning literature and journalism, and becoming a bicycle instructor. I calculate that with fees and tips—and I am told that good-looking young men, possessed of agreeable manners and a knowledge of flirtation, receive a good deal in the way of tips—and the lending of machines worth five pounds to the English aristocracy at three shillings an hour, I can secure an income of from thirty to forty thousand a year. Promenading a park, with my arm round a pretty girl's waist, is, I feel, the vocation for which nature intended me. The business would be less harassing than my present employment. The only thing I should miss would be the criticism. Next time I write to you, I shall probably address my letter from "The *To-day* Bicycling School," or from the office of "*The Idler* Bicycling Club for Young Ladies."

In the days when I learnt bicycling, three lessons at the most were considered necessary to a would-be rider. The bicycle—a depressed-looking machine, hired at the rate of sixpence for the first hour and threepence for every hour afterwards—was led in triumph from its shed. You scrambled up on to it, and Tom on one side, and Dick on the other, pushed you gently along towards the crown of the hill. Our instructors did not assure us that they would not let us go, that they would hold us up at all hazards and keep us safe. They said,—

"Now we're going to give you a shove, so look out," and they did it, and down the hill one went, shouting, "I'll punch your head, Tommy Steggles, when I get you." "All right, Dickey Jones, you'll be sorry for this." But the only response we obtained was the sound of laughter growing fainter, mingled with such encouraging cries as "Go it, legs! Have you got any sticking-plaster?"

At the bottom of the hill there lay grass, upon which a gentleman might fall with ease and comfort, comparatively speaking, and in the distance, one solitary heap of stones. You might have thought it difficult for an inexperienced rider to make direct for those stones. You might think he would have fallen before he reached them. There must have been magnets in some of them, or there must have existed a secret understanding between them and the bicycle. At one moment it looked as if the rider might get past them, but the stones would call to him, "This way, please, you have got to come. Better get it over." And then with a quick and clever turn he would dash towards them. But, as I said, on the third morning he could ride.

PUSHKIN PRESS—THE LONDON LIBRARY

"FOUND ON THE SHELVES"

1   *Cycling: The Craze of the Hour*
2   *The Lure of the North*
3   *On Corpulence: Feeding the Body and Feeding the Mind*
4   *Life in a Bustle: Advice to Youth*
5   *The Gentlewoman's Book of Sports*
6   *On Reading, Writing and Living with Books*

FORTHCOMING:

7   *Through a Glass Lightly: Confession of a Reluctant
    Water Drinker*
8   *The Right to Fly*
9   *The Noble English Art of Self-Defence*
10 *Hints on Etiquette: A Shield Against the Vulgar*
11 *A Woman's Walks*
12 *A Full Account of the Dreadful Explosion of Wallsend
    Colliery by which 101 Human Beings Perished!*

THE LONDON LIBRARY (a registered charity) is one of the UK's leading literary institutions and a favourite haunt of authors, researchers and keen readers.

Membership is open to all.

Join at www.londonlibrary.co.uk.

www.pushkinpress.com